Do You Expect Your Art to Answer?

❧

Laurel S. Peterson

FUTURECYCLE PRESS
www.futurecycle.org

Cover artwork, Amazon *by David Burt, photographed
by Ralph Adams; author photo by Ute-Christin Photography,
LLC; cover and interior book design by Diane Kistner;
Caxton text and titling*

Library of Congress Control Number: 2016961833

Published by FutureCycle Press
Lexington, Kentucky, USA

ISBN 978-1-942371-22-9

Contents

*For Van, who helps me slow down and look,
and for Alison, wonderful friend, who shared
the experience of the Whitney Biennial
where it all began*

Little Girl

for Nabokov

You drive me crazy
demanding a bone
curling into
the hollow throat
of my arms
where I swallow you
again and again

Late October

Childe Hassam, Golden Afternoon,
Metropolitan Museum of Art

Through the Indian Summer window,
dead leaves float their smell
and her five-year-old self, riding in on it,
demands to be unyoked
from knowledge:
those dead leaves,
their dry paper,
the fracturing of their delicate spines.

Symphony In White No. 1: The White Girl

*James McNeill Whistler, National Gallery of Art,
Washington, DC*

We see only the skin of her hands and face
under her high-collared dress,
its paleness curtaining her body
from neck to floor.
Beneath her feet,
a wolf's head watches,
mouth open, teeth exposed.

No blood stains the white;
the violence is long past,
her unruly hair
the only evidence.

Sfumato

*In art, indicating vague outlines and a generally
hazy or smoky appearance; said of a painting*

In this half dark,
the waking world
looks different,
sounds new.
In the distance, the hum
of movement—
highways slowly crowding,
air heating with jet exhaust,
the thick grumble of diesel
engines pulling away
from the dock.

Edges blur, as if from low light
filtered through trees,
light that doesn't yet
know what it is,
how to fill itself out
into day

whose bright hardness shaves off
the down of our apprehension,
forces us into frames,
portraits of ourselves,
sturdy, precise,
desperately clear.

This smoky birth
promises that forms
evaporate into each other,
that edges are edges only
when we draw lines,
and you are the end
of the middle
of where I begin.

Pre-Christian Burial

Masters of Fire: Copper Age Art from Israel,
Institute for the Study of the Ancient World,
New York University, March 2014

He was made to be broken.

Of red clay,
elongated torso, stubs of legs,
hollow—I can see the light
through his eyes.

Shattered before interment,
he's been resurrected,
bits of neutral earth
cementing the fragments
into a whole
red like blood,
red like the copper earth.

Chadri

Gift of Diana Vreeland, 1972, to the Metropolitan Museum of Art (20th century, Afghan culture, medium: cotton and silk)

The white one fronts the red one
that fronts a black void.
Voluminous folds shroud
manikins that could be male
or female—who cares without
the voluptuous flow of skin?

Men aren't required to give up their faces,
their bodies, for fashion, for decorum,
just because a woman might lose her self-control
and with a knife, a gun, her weighted muscles,
demand he strip so she can sink her fingernails,
her knife tip, into his naked skin.

Woman

[Street Scene: Exhausted Woman Seated on Stoop], New York City, Leon Levinstein, Metropolitan Museum of Art

She sat on steps
at the edge of the avenue,
half in the light of day,
half in the light of evening,
her shoulders bent like osteoporosis,
bones compacting into stone dust.

People keep handing me things, she said.
At first, a half-filled coffee cup,
a plate with a little leftover fruit.
Could you clean these? they ask.
Wash them and tuck them
where we can't see them anymore.

Then, the things got bigger.
They handed me their cheating husbands,
their children's empty beer cans and stolen goods,
their parents' beatings and curses,
their dead friends.

Me, she said, *I'm still carrying that coffee cup,*
looking for a place to put it down,
to put it all down.

Her arms and legs shone dark against the white-painted stairs.

Ernesta (Child with Nurse)

Cecilia Beaux, Metropolitan Museum of Art

Little girl, cheeks scrubbed, brown silk hair:
In her white dress and rose hat,
she watches us watching her,
her hand firmly clasped by her nurse.

She doesn't know yet what it's like to have a man
force her against a brick wall in the dark.
His breath smokes in her mouth,
his chipped tooth snatches blood from her bottom lip,
his hands write his story on her skin.

She doesn't know yet
that he's returned from Afghanistan
(or Iraq or Vietnam or prison),
having shot a child, the child's mother,
escaped a sniper, an IED, a raging father,
that all he wants is comfort
but his only remaining language is violence.

Nude in the Bath

A painting by Pierre Bonnard

Fragments of light, floor tiles,
the bare outline of a towel.

Like Charlene who's being divorced
and can't sell her art, giant squares
of flowers and tropical birds
in hot pink and neon green,
and she is angry.

She had everything: a stockbroker
husband who bought her an SUV to haul
those canvases to galleries, and every morning
she woke to a studio he designed for her
bordered by windows that framed
chlorophyll greenery and the spiciness
of pink peonies and pool chlorine.

No one ever knows what really happens.
Drop the curtain, it's dark in there.

In the painting, the woman's belly is wrinkled,
her breasts a Mediterranean blue.
A small red streak blurs on the tub's edge,
and the water, it fractures left, right and center,
rising.

How Love Disappears

All his photographs focus
on vanishing points:
the road that flees
into the flat New Mexican desert,
the Brooklyn Bridge departing
toward the Twin Towers.

And in the small Italian village
where he spent eight months learning
to etch copper plates, a man's shadow stretches
toward a darkened house
where his wife and child linger,
diminishing as it goes.

Persephone

Mary Frank, 1987, Bruce Museum,
Greenwich, CT

Bronze blued now by rain, heat,
she writhes up in liquid pieces from her ivy bed,
eyes closed, as if light could blind her.
Coming back is so hard.

It takes her weeks to reassemble,
find her wholeness,
always swimming upwards from under
as if from drugged sleep,
her skin reshaping to her bones,
her fingers grasping, again, her life.

Waking

Schlafende Frau (Sleeping Woman) *from the series*
Die Träumenden Knaben (The Dreaming Boys),
Oskar Kokoschka, Color Lithograph, Illustration,
Metropolitan Museum of Art

Sleep's a shallow test grave,
descent into suffocating black
absence, a dirty taste of eternity's loss.
Expanded lungs
exhale toward heat and light
the empty black dreams
and silent groans of other dead.
Then night's disjointing departs,
its soiled edges crumbling as daylight presses in.

Erasures

Prayers for Songs Unheard *by Charlotte Hedlund*

Ink and collage on board,
barest impression of mallard,
head bent back,
neck exposed.
Behind the floating bird
in this half world,
mauve water
separates into its past—
pale blue, cream, red—
its purple shadow fading
into the darkening paper.

Lonely,
the faintest pencil line
contours the bird,
present, but disappearing, like us.

The throat terrifies,
vulnerable,
supplicant beak raised like that
below a hole into which
its silence flows.
Wings folded,
down rendered soft as prayer.

If the beak would open,
if the music we wished for come forth.
Then, aching.

Augury

Henry Ray Abrams' photograph of black smoke pouring from the World Trade Center Towers, September 11 (Getty Images)

Light the color of cold butter
sits on the blue dish of horizon.
I'm lonely at your death
which haunts me
without being.
I'm lonely for what we might have had,
which is still possible.

Yesterday, I rode the train
into New York with the thin
cincture of CNN binding me
like nylon fishing line:
Al Qaeda threatens U.S. railways.

Now, double bands of butter stripe
the evening sky, blue smoke between:
November's colors and all of November
descend with their cool, damp weight.
The sky explodes pink
like spores from a puffball.

Valentino: *Elle,* Page 48

Pale pointed leather toes,
sparkles that slide up the ankle
like three-tiered
razor wire
topping a fortress wall.

Legs disappear
into chiffon pleats
and a rivet-studded
chiffon wrap.
No one can see her
knees behind their skirt curtain.

She's just standing there—
In a museum? At the bus stop?
In her foyer?—
waiting for her chauffeur to escort her
to the ball, because sure as hell
she's not walking anywhere.
She's perfectly still,
though the picture is blurred,
as if my turning the page
shook the camera,
sent all the pixels flying
one dot to the left.

It Speaks

"148 Ripples-Reef" by Chris Perry at the Rowayton
Art Gallery, Rowayton, CT, September 2016

Without language, lonely isn't something
I comprehend.
I know it only because my edges
are sharply sliced,
knifing the gallery air.

Beware of me.
You think you can see through me,
but it's only a hollow in my meaning.
The rest is contained in darkness,
squared away between cardboard covers,
lost in white.

The Great Divide

[Doorway Into Crumbling Brick Building]
(Photograph, 1850s), Artist unknown,
Metropolitan Museum of Art

Her outside is majestic:
a swathe of butterscotch brick,
her shanks punctuated by rectangular eyes.
If you look deep enough,
you see her pitted steel ribs.
A rusty band binds her forehead
under a graying roof gently dusted
with white.
She is foursquare solid,
a great mammoth of density;
the force of her age seems more
than the glaze it is.

Inside, she is dim.
Her expansive corners have piled
up dust to hide their sharp edges.
The girders are melting,
the mortar curdles between the bricks.
She is lonely, haunted, unused,
feels the lack of her education.
No one told her how it would feel
to be discarded.

Hansel

In response to a painting by Åsa Antalffy Eriksson

The child has found the door in the woods—
he of the rust and green earth,
his hood tipped back as if to catch
the brilliant feather that prowls above him,
a feather as opaque as he is translucent.
Light like a promise of white-hot heaven
streams through the trees
and the door.

Oh, child of mine,
child I never bore,
be wary.
Already you are disappearing,
your hands invisible
in the fairy wood.

Listen to me:
On the other side, everything is the same
—and nothing is. The light enchants,
but light always enchants,
promising us sight. But light
will erase you.

You'll step. You can't help it.
Nothing can stop you.

But, oh.
Who abandoned you here,
in this empty wood,
this empty world,
where the only choice is forward?

What Grandmother Said

After a portrait of Julia Margaret Cameron
by Henry Herschel Hay Cameron, 1870,
Metropolitan Museum of Art

And there, it's gone,
a flourish of hours,
paper-thin and light,
floating on a breeze so faint
we don't feel its stealth.

How does it happen?
How do we lose so easily,
setting the moment aside,
in favor of pursuit?

Night Image of Chicago

NASA Image of the Day, April 13, 2016

Observed from the International Space Station,
Chicago at night looks like a golden hog
with a flopped over ear—a hog, I grant you,
gridded and shimmering with a million lights:
cars, streetlights, neon, phones, lamps,
the lonely speck of a lighter.

All roads lead to the lake shore,
a black wash against the pig's back,
where a lilac cloud dangles over Navy Pier.
Maybe it's an amethyst set in the gold.
Maybe it's fractured light.
Maybe it's the city's eye.

All my life, I have loved high places:
the uplift of the jet,
the swing of the Ferris wheel,
the rocky tip of the mountain path.
From there, I can *see,*
maybe even all the way to a horizon.
If you were one of those specks of light and looked up,
you wouldn't even know I was here.

Infinity Space

Doug Wheeler, SA MI 75 DZ NY 12,
David Zwirmer Gallery, New York City,
January 17 to February 25, 2012

A shifting mimicry
of rising sun and spreading dark
moves across white and white—
walls that melt into floors
or ceiling, disappearing
without edges
corners
ends—
blinding, nauseating
in its emptiness.

Who are we kidding?
We love that unease,
its temporary promise of forever.
On the cold stone gallery floor,
we stand safely outside it,
looking in,
a long line of spectators
craving the light.

Threnody

In honor of Cleve Gray's beautiful painting series,
The Neuberger Museum, Purchase College,
Purchase, NY

Its monumental figures refuse me,
surround me in this cathedral.
The shadows writhe
while one red figure flames
in this theater to the dead,
of the dead,
theirs and ours,
then and now.

Shimmering black, sacred space.
Here, all the colors
of longing and lamentation
spark and explode
among our darknesses.

Empty Cathedrals

All through Europe, she visited
cathedrals, medieval man's
stone, wood and glass prayer
to his god, the god
that ended that age
with the Black Death.

She went for the mosaics that stretched for yards
across floors and up walls like quilted light;
for rose windows and marble carvings;
for the keystone that locked together the ribs of the roof;
for the clerestory, whose window illuminated
the cathedral's central space; for the spire that shot
toward heaven from the cross of nave and transept;
because these promised
raw heat, penetration.

Some days she dragged her fingertips
across those stones and hoped
one living bacterium would leap
to infect her; at least then
her body would hold something.

But the majestic spaces offered only
transept bisecting nave, tombs behind gilded bars,
the arches flying between buttress and pier,
piers like God's canes on the cathedral floor,
and crucifixions glowing in glass.

And the god that might have been there only
shuddered faintly through ruby panes
like shadowy leaves.

This afternoon, the sun colors
an echoing nave.
She sits drenched in topaz hoping
to be warmed, fingertips tented—
            here's the church,
            here's the steeple—
ever empty except
for the hope that, past
what she believes,
magic may answer.

In the Glass House

At the New Orleans Museum of Art

All morning spent
with the organic lines of Tiffany and Chilhuly,
the practical curves of Cambridge East and Sandwich,
compotes with their curling lips,
opalescent celery jars, pocked roemers,
pressed cup plates, droppers, goblets,
and a Robert Willson armadillo.

While she meditates in front
of an amphora from 25 A.D.,
awed that Christ lived
when that vase poured from the fire,
a group of boys
no more than fourteen, fifteen,
saunters through with a docent
and a Department of Corrections guard—
a burly man in blue—
and all she can think is
what did they do to be in and
what did they do to be out?

They listen quietly, checking out titles,
marveling how minerals in mud
where the ancient glass fell
charmed it with color
where it had before been clear.

Are we all transparent at the start?

Here in the glass house,
this sacred space, these intimate
cloth-walled rooms, the light dimly gleams
on the flaws that make beauty.

The Chinese Garden Court

Metropolitan Museum of Art,
Shan-shui (landscape):
water and mountain drawn together

Time and again,
we repair to this room
or this room repairs us—
or could if small children
didn't clamber over
the stone benches
and stick their fingers
into *Deep Green Jade Spring*
to toy with the goldfish.

Now across the Taihu rocks,
piled in peaks, they drag
their baby fingers, then swing
around the Nan wood columns,
an evergreen valued
to near extinction.
Here comes the guard;
the parents startle
like newborn calves.

What would the scholar-gentlemen
who conceived these spaces
for *Go* and music and quiet conversation

say to those two little blonds,
in their matching pink shirts?

Would they puncture the silence with shouts
like the sudden sharp bark
of a dog at a stranger?
Would they celebrate the childish voices,
the guard's remonstrance,
the city's rumbling purr?

Or would they frown,
as silent and austere as a calligraphic scroll,
seeking the perfect harmony
with which we credit them
because our own longing is
as vast as the mountain,
as vast as the joyful water.

Dans le Musée Picasso Paris

A sunburned horse
on a step by an empty sea
presses a key
to a door with no keyhole.

You think Picasso posed his horse
like one of Hopper's women,
islanded in light and color.
You think his monochromatic flesh dull,
his body mere abstraction, his isolation
to be pitied amidst that wash of Brittany blue
and sepia. You dissect
his futility, the fingerprints
of the palette knife, his lonely nose,

and he turns his eyes on you,
shocked at the cruelty
of your surgical gaze.

Celadon

Liu Jianhua, Container Series
Definition from Art Gallery of NSW, January 2015:
"full moon dyed with spring water"

It is the color of Korean pottery,
of your eyes first thing on a winter morning, the sun
shining on the sheets like a glaze of ice;
the color of spring rain,
of the light through the first spring leaves;
it's the color of late afternoon loneliness,
the color of Vaseline glass—almost.
The bowl on my desk holds pale stones washed
by the celadon Caribbean sea.

Liu Jianhua's Container Series pours ruby
into celadon—pitchers, bowls, platters,
cups offered up to our consumptive
gaze, as if we were drinking
another life, eating another body,
a demented communion,
the color of love as it ebbs away,
the color of love as it's given.

In Quimper

It's a pottery town—
mercantile—
French mixed with Celtic,
home of Arthurian legends,
out here in the blue and white
light of Brittany.

It's misting
so we hesitate on our way to dinner
for a painted landscape glowing
in a previously shuttered gallery.

Mostly white with thin black lines
islanded in the purity,
the paintings are complemented with poems.
Poets ourselves,
we pause to translate:

L'amiel. What's that? I ask
of my Francophile husband.
We don't know, and neither does Google Translate.
Just inside, the poet, his head wild with cirrus white hair,
drinks champagne with his painter friend.

L'amiel, he enthuses, his hands
waving his glass across the crowded interior.
I made it up!

La mer = sea; le ciel = sky,
and where they slide into one another,
where the line disappears—that's l'amiel!
He grins.

We grin.
He pours us champagne—
and in two languages,
three with gestures, we talk
of art's power to convey spirit,
of how it raises us to joy, to forgiveness,
so the line between artist and God disappears.

Champagne drunk,
we drift on a bubbly high
to eat giant plates of crustaceans—
just us now.
My husband employs Google once more:
Who is this poet?
President of a royalist party
linked to Action Française, fascist,
those who, in the 1930s, supported the Nazis.

Black and white, the islands float.

Cuenca Sunday

What I remember are extravagant
Spanish voices cracking
off hard white walls
in the Museo de Arte Abstracto Español.
Floor-to-ceiling windows
curtained with a snowfall
of chiffon barely held back
bleached Spanish sunshine
and the gorge's sharp visage,
cold light on cold stone.
Later at lunch,
we would watch climbers
attempt the chasm's
crescent moon overhang
and fail.

The medieval city is piled up high,
but the modern, scattered at its base,
dusty and tawdry like the long skirts
of a flamenco dancer,
shutters against its Sunday visitors.
Its old spirit hides in the hill,
packed about by rock,
silent in the cold block of the Gothic cathedral,
absent from the abstract
black slashes, slabs of cool yellow
or agitated lines on white canvas.

We came yearning
for Muslim conquerors and St. Julian,
for textiles and monks hunched
over vellum, but they were dust
long before we arrived,
and the harsh open light revealed
only the empty mirrors of our own selves.

Buddha Selfies

TV Buddha, *Nam June Paik (1976),*
Art Gallery NSW, Sydney, Australia

"As the wooden figure timelessly contemplates a
live image of itself watching, the TV screen becomes
the unexpected site for a reflection or reincarnation
of the Buddha."

There he sits: Buddha.
The curator intones that the TV camera is
an unexpected site for a...reincarnation of the Buddha,
like somehow the camera makes him infinite,
a god's eye—which is god? which god is it?—
looking at himself
looking at himself
and looking at us
looking at him
while we look at ourselves,
our favorite thing,
snapping selfies
and pictures of the pictures
in museums
so we can post them
for others to admire (us)
admiring the Buddha
admiring himself.

So maybe in 1976
reincarnation was unexpected,
but today it's like blowflies on a dead body.
A woman poses her designer legs
next to the Buddha. His fingers press his chest,
cracking and chipped,
the black heart of the camera.
Like her, he cannot resist
staring at his beautiful, infinite,
technological self.

The Meaning of Ritual

A response to Passover *by Suzanne Benton*

Once, we ate Passover dinner
with your late wife's family.
I knew nothing of bitter herbs
or unleavened bread,
only of the lamb later transformed
into my Easter's sacrifice.

On this illuminated manuscript,
the feast sprawls
below the bloody lintel,
rusty pyramid of slavery,
crimson border of exclamation points
like the walls of the split Red Sea.

Why does God pass over?
What ritual saves us?
The purifying search for chametz
with feather, candle and spoon?
Body and blood in wafer and wine?
Your wife, she's gone,
taken by cancer,
your mother-in-law
still furious with grief.

Our loss of each other,
implied by time, is staved off
only by nightly feasts
and the bloody lintel
of our denial.

What I'd Take from the Fire

"Light rains that fell overnight helped calm the
Waldo Canyon Fire, which has scorched 28 square
miles, killed two and destroyed almost 350 homes."
Source: msnbc.com.

That clichés are true:
You can't go home again.
The river is the same
but not
over that rock that is the same
but imperceptibly smaller
than when you read this line.

That what you love isn't really
what you love;
it's what it means.
That loneliness never leaves us.

I saw the fire
and the fire saw me.
The fire decided it owned me.
The fire decided its path;
whimsy and the breeze
helped it forage for fuel.
The fire consumed me
even as it left my
blackened bones to whiten.

What I take from the fire is this:
The fire belongs
to the gods of war—
the raging, slaughtering,
blood-in-the-nose-and-mouth gods
of revenge and chastisement,
vampire gods that suck your children's blood
and spit it whole into the salty sea.

What I take from the fire are lost prayers
ascending in acres of smoke
over sacrifices of golden bone and silver flesh,
over questions and answers burned
with equal abandon.

The American with the Camera

Theodore Nierenberg: Photographs from
His World Travels, *Bruce Museum, Greenwich, CT*

What is your life? Who are you, girl
with the marmalade can perched on your head,
yellow beads decorating your neck,
and that smile?

Who are you, brothers, fishing there in your boat,
smoke rising from its edge?
What are you burning in the boat,
each of you at one end, like a balance
in that wide expanse of silver-gray water?
How am I to know you
from just one image? And yet—

I see your turquoise earring,
your necklace of shells and glass,
your carved spear or pipe (I cannot tell which,
even though I look closely),
how carefully your hair is parted,
and that thin line of it along your brow—
who did that for you?—
and I make a story:
Someone gave you that earring
and taught you to look coyly
up through your lashes
at the American with the camera.

Do you mind that your image was captured
to be hung where you may never see it?
Would you look at my photograph
if it were hung in your world?
Can our stories touch
as I look into your eyes?

Yellow Ribbon

Gateway to Norwalk, *Sculpture,*
West Avenue, Norwalk, CT

It traverses the wall, a looping yellow steel vine,
kin to the honeysuckle across the street,
not a gate so much as the path of an arrow
made visible, dragging us forward,
both movement and stillness,
words and silence between words,
here and elsewhere,
us and other.

Bienvenue, shanti, soledad, peace—
its languages unscroll,
slipping and twirling into the leaves and grass,
defiant under the thundering highways,
a tone poem that sings of selves beyond divisions.

Driving away, I see a woman alone,
dark hair looping down her back,
who meets the transport-for-disabled van
in the liquor store parking lot.
As I wait for the light to change,
she lifts her school-aged son
from his seat and carries him
up the hill toward home.

Oyster Shell Park

Trucks on I-95 rumble
at my back,
and the river stretches
at my feet. A lone
fisherman slaps fish heads,
eyes still glistening,
onto his hook.
Clots of scullers glide through the water,
their coach berating
from her megaphone
like a skeet shooter: *pull, pull, pull.*
Two railroad-tie-and-iron sculptures
depict hangings.
Behind me a new row of trees,
one for each soul shot
at Newtown.
The wind off the waves
blows up salt.
It tastes like blood.

Portrait I

So Marta, the woman who shared a hallway with me
at the school where I met my husband before his wife died;
she who down the hall one day was weeping
because she and her lover had broken
again, he to return to his wife
and she to the quiet apartment she shared
with their thirty-year affair.
I wasn't to tell; I was never to tell,
a skill I was already versed in
having grown up in a house where shadows
stretched across the afternoons.

For Marta, there was almost a child once, a flight
to Puerto Rico before such things were legal,
a dead brother, parents for whom she cared as they lingered,
stalling her PhD, still unfinished, entangled again and again with him.
And now, near seventy, she teaches writing part-time, as always,
and reads intelligent books over vegetable dinners with wine
off the grid upstate in a farmhouse, hair long and silver,
her small, precise fingers flickering over a page of text.
At least this is how I imagine her, since we lost touch years ago:
quiet, reading, captured by Wyeth or Hopper, perhaps
looking out the window at an empty field.

Portrait II

My Aunt Carolyn, the last time I saw her, warned me not to stand
too close to the microwave because the ELFs caused cancer,
this as she heated a bag to clutch after the chemotherapy
for her lungs shrunk her to a stick.
Later, she held my hand and told me
she wanted me with her at the pearly gates
where she said all the aunties were waiting.
Two years now she's been gone.

Oh, Auntie, I hope your pearly gates glisten with jewels
and that you have found forgiveness
for all your unnamed sins—and mine.
That your glorious soprano is singing in God's choir,
and, if that's where we all end up,
I'll be there with you, at least painted in the background,
like the girl with her hair in a braid
in Henry Lerolle's *The Organ Rehearsal,*
watching you at the balcony's edge
in your funny hat, a little worse for the wear,
singing to the sheer white light.

After Your Dying, I Am What Remains

For Hindemith, Sonata for Solo Viola (No. 2),
P. 25, No. 1 (1922)

I & II

I sit in the darkening afternoon,
the cat pacing around me,
tense for her feeding,
music scratching at ears, nose, eyes,
and the snow falls,
and the falling of it obliterates the landscape
and memory is obliterated with it
as you also are being sucked under the cold
wet blanket
of dying
and I am left alone to manage
your afterlife
and I cannot.

III

Lost in this silvery afternoon
are the haunted moments when faith abounded—
when we could still hear
past your screams
and my tears
and the new puppy made tomorrow seem possible

Where are you?

All has gone black,
has become a space of strafed skin,
burnt edges, rough stone,
and the impatient calling
of other women who caress my bones
and cart yours away
in small neat baskets while I weep
over each, nurturing your last dry remains
with my tears,
a few for each basket
so each may sprout a new woman.

For all the hate we mixed in our love,
I am so lonely without you.

I carry you in me in regret,
piecemeal, a joint of your finger in my hip,
your belly curled in my neck muscles,
the dark strands of your hair twisted
across my throat.

IV

Then you were gone,
suddenly, a flash of light,
not even a movement or a cry.
Your soul hovered
a few wing shudders, rapid
and contained, flimsy,
and before I could say good-bye,

the crowds arrived and crowded and sympathized
and pressed flowers on me
and fed me sandwiches and Scotch
and hovered like your soul hovered,
ever present in the background,
a hum and buzz
under all the hum and buzz
of the hysteria of
burning and burying you
and the crowds crowding around
with their perfume and eyes
and hot breath and incessant
living selves.

V

Back in the darkening afternoon:
More light has slipped
from my grasp into
the timelessness of tomorrow
where somehow I may find you.

Longing will speed me there
yet I am loathe to finish
what little light may yet be mine.
Not because I don't long for you
but perhaps because
the dying light may be
all there is of you.

The Intruder

Every week,
I send a card. This one holds
a poem about singing,
breathing, Rothko.

She says they help—
something to look toward,
a not-darkness in the darkness.

But it's just paper and words,
barely enough to feed a match;
not enough to get a heart started
or burn away the intruder.

Holiday Train Show

New York Botanical Garden, December 2013

It's hard to enter delight,
even at Christmas,
even surrounded
by miniature trains of leaves and bark
chugging through a fairyland
of magical houses conjured from dried flowers
and twigs, the 59th Street Bridge in branches
and tiny blue flames
above our heads.

Elsewhere, red and white glittering lights
wrap living trees.
Evergreens upthrust against heaven,
stars at their crowns,
boast branches heavy with floating
sleighs and fat elves.
Luminous around them,
hand-blown spheres bob
in cobalt and burgundy,
emerald and milk.
Outside, the hope of snowmen
floats gently to the ground.

Under the same canopy of white
lives a man in his truck,

tucked into woods just far enough
that the dog knows he's there.
He's a thief, our neighbor says,
distributing holiday party invitations.

And across the country, a mother lies
dying, frantic in her hospital
bed: *Don't leave me here.*
White and red lights blink around her,
the monitors' soft beeping
her Christmas music.

Spirits of the House

*For Billy Collins, who once said in a reading that
we could never be too grateful that inanimate
things remained inanimate*

The television is, of course, female.
What else could hold a man entranced for hours?
The bookshelves are male,
ponderous, heavy with abstraction,
linear, their blocky lines
cross-wording the wall.
The laptop wears a long, flowing pink dress,
has red hair. She is the daughter
of Aphrodite and Thor.
Mother Goddess nestles in the couch:
fertility of snack crumbs,
small beads and loose change;
plump, embracing arms welcome you to sleep.
The mobile above the baby's bed
holds the spirit of the air,
a slow-motion tease.

And Maggie the Cat—little dark soul
who keeps the rest in line—patrols,
egregiously matted and unsteady,
her once beautiful tortoiseshell fur
now a used car lot of dried food and feces.
She alone stands between us and the poltergeists
winging disorder through the house,

they who would rearrange the books,
sneak silverware into the underwear drawer,
move themselves—couch, television, bookshelf—
to the other side of the room at midnight
to wound an unwary householder,
make phone calls to an old lover,
hypnotize a man so he forgets his life.

James Mollison: The Disciples

Aldrich Contemporary Art Museum, Ridgefield, CT,
November 13, 2013

It's not just their clothes but their expressions:
raging defiance on The Casualties' fans' faces
whose clothing bleeds the excessive
patterning of a baronial house
inherited for twenty generations,
tartans and plaids and studs and ammo belts
and ripped fishnets and leather and patches and medallions.
Their hair stands in Lady Liberty spikes,
stoplight green, rocket red,
faces of stone-carved fury,
feet apart in fighting stances, except for fat guy,
who looks as if he's ready to cry, and pouty guy,
who looks as if he's scratching his butt.

The P. Diddy group wears black,
the women's breasts barely restrained by crochet or lace,
skirts at their crotches, thighs shiny and thick;
for the men big pants, big shirts, wide ties,
anything to cover their underfed frames.
Their faces pantomime sultry: *What is sultry?*
Does it look like this?

The only group smiling is The Wailers' fans
in their green, yellow and red stripes and Rasta hair,

while the Bob Dylan fans in their long wool coats
and scarves are draped with the same gray exhaustion
as the Merle Haggard fans in their overalls and denim shirts.

And the women for Bjork, Icelandic electronics witch
whose voice haunts like wind down fjords,
wear their pale loneliness in overdressed layers—
furs and scarves, lace collars, bows and frills and ruffles—
their bird-fine faces
turned toward you.

Whitney Biennial: 2012

Last night at the preview,
when the pipe organ bellowed
its timbre of missile tubes,
when the goo on the floor waved
its black tentacles in a fanned breeze,
ominous, primordial;

last night when we went from the room
of the undiagnosed paranoid schizophrenic
who cut a hole in his penis to let god in
to the room about soul
where music yelled and bruised
and images unrolled on screens like old maps
drawn with dragons and sea monsters;

when we viewed vaginas
cut up the middle with scissors,
a video of a woman regurgitating her food
into a bowl, when we walked through empty
almost-rooms, scrim of water molding
in the almost-shower-stall;

last night when the patron in plaid tie and jeans
demanded of a dark-eyed artist displayed in her atelier,
when he insisted like an assault that she

DO SOMETHING:
What's this supposed to be anyway?

When she asked him:
Do you expect your art to answer?

Witness

Lust is tattooed on his smooth
forearm—perhaps so he won't forget
he has it. Stranger to stranger,
he tells me
on a gold-tipped afternoon
sitting atop Met steps stippled
with tourists
that he is one in New York
of maybe five
who can   rollerblade
            down
        these steps
backwards.

Somewhere else in the city that afternoon,
another young man with another tattoo
backhands another woman
with a razor and makes the seventeenth page
of the Metro section.
I respect my fear of this
and have arrived on these steps
zipped into denim,
not linen,
as if that weighted millimeter would save me
from being female.

Into that lingering late light will come
the friend for whom I wait. We'll ascend
to a planked roof garden
planted with Ellsworth Kelly sculptures
and drink wine until the sun
explodes over the Dakota and goes out
for the evening in her black gown.

For most of our conversation,
a young lawyer—I have made him
a lawyer although he could be anything—
will stand behind my friend and watch me
and the sunset in his ink-blue shirt.

The blader tells me he'll prove his claim
as soon as the museum guards finish
their smoke break.
He waits, skating figure eights
on the platform that tops the stairs.
The guards vanish. The steps clear.
He builds up his speed,
twists into reverse,
and hurtles toward the plaza,
his body leaning up toward
the museum in a fluid longing
to escape the injury implicit
in his misstep.
The wheels clatter his progress,

he watches his back:
                        third tier,
                second tier,
            first tier,
plaza.

A pirouette and he's gone.
Safe.

At the National Portrait Gallery

Canberra, ACT, Australia

Patrick Corrigan, freight entrepreneur and arts benefactor, stands
in his portrait like that guy Charlene once knew who would blow
into town for a quickie: business and a shag. Charlene was his
midlife crisis, dressed up in lipstick like blood, black skirt like a
bandage. She'd babysat his daughters, asked after his wife.
He'd look at art to humor her, take her to eat lobster and drink
champagne, remind her Jesus is an historical fact, then take her
back to his room at the Yale Club.

Corrigan's penthouse walls are covered with art—objects he prizes
like that guy prized Charlene, like a new racing yacht or a small
Picasso. Hands in pockets, belly bulging in its double-breasted
jacket, he is a man of red wine and steak, of shrimp with butter,
of collections. He stares out of the canvas as if, even inanimate,
it's all his to take.

In Solesme

a ninety-year-old woman
climbed on her bike after Vespers
and cycled into the softening French dusk,
the sunlight of all her years gathered
into bones that pedaled and prayed
in the church of the monastery
whose sleek stone walls
rose up from the river Sarthe.
Who was she to carry such lightness
in the face of that grandeur?

A James Kohler Rug

In Santa Fe, the horizon stretches
to the next gallery: paintings, rugs, jewelry—
the landscape beyond dominated
by sandstone and scrub pine.

How do I tell you about the rug?
The James Kohler that got away,
a cobalt, black and white Indian mask
with six feet by four of perfect selvages.

His weaver's soul was in there, too,
hooked in like weft into warp,
a little more with each thread.

And here's the point,
see, I'm getting to it:
The Navajos, they leave a little hole
in their rugs for the soul's escape,
just one little space
that opens wide into heaven.

Acknowledgments

Grateful acknowledgement goes to the editors of the following publications, in which these poems first appeared, sometimes in earlier versions:

Ekphrastic.net: "Nude in the Bath"
Pinyon: "Little Girl"
Prairie Winds: "Empty Cathedrals"
Verse-Virtual: "Celadon," "Chadri," "Portrait I," "Portrait II,"
    "Threnody," "Waking Slow," "Woman"

"After Your Dying, I Am What Remains" first appeared in
That's the Way the Music Sounds by Laurel S. Peterson (Finishing Line Press, 2009).

"Woman" appears in *Laureates of Connecticut: An Anthology of Contemporary Poetry,* Ginny Lowe Connors and Charlie Margolis, Eds. Grayson, 2017.

"Erasures" was written for a Words in Art project at Silvermine Gallery, Norwalk, CT, where it was also presented in 2010. "Yellow Ribbon" was written for the July 13, 2016, opening and dedication of the Gateway to Norwalk art work to the town of Norwalk, CT, in the author's role as poet laureate.

Permission to photograph the statue *Amazon* by David Burt was granted by Mr. Jeffrey Mueller, Gallery Director, of the Silvermine Art Center (New Canaan, CT).

A special thanks to Elizabeth Beck for her assistance with the cover photo.

About FutureCycle Press

FutureCycle Press is dedicated to publishing lasting English-language poetry books, chapbooks, and anthologies in both print-on-demand and Kindle ebook formats. Founded in 2007 by long-time independent editor/publishers and partners Diane Kistner and Robert S. King, the press incorporated as a nonprofit in 2012. A number of our editors are distinguished poets and writers in their own right, and we have been actively involved in the small press movement going back to the early seventies.

The FutureCycle Poetry Book Prize and honorarium is awarded annually for the best full-length volume of poetry we publish in a calendar year. Introduced in 2013, our Good Works projects are anthologies devoted to issues of universal significance, with all proceeds donated to a related worthy cause. Our Selected Poems series highlights contemporary poets with a substantial body of work to their credit; with this series we strive to resurrect work that has had limited distribution and is now out of print.

We are dedicated to giving all of the authors we publish the care their work deserves, making our catalog of titles the most diverse and distinguished it can be, and paying forward any earnings to fund more great books.

We've learned a few things about independent publishing over the years. We've also evolved a unique, resilient publishing model that allows us to focus mainly on vetting and preserving for posterity poetry collections of exceptional quality without becoming overwhelmed with bookkeeping and mailing, fundraising activities, or taxing editorial and production "bubbles." Come see us at www.futurecycle.org to find out more.

The FutureCycle Poetry Book Prize

All full-length volumes of poetry published by FutureCycle Press in a given calendar year are considered for the annual FutureCycle Poetry Book Prize. This allows us to consider each submission on its own merits, outside of the context of a contest. Too, the judges see the finished book, which will have benefitted from the beautiful book design and strong editorial gloss we are famous for.

The book ranked the best in judging is announced as the prize-winner in the subsequent year. There is no fixed monetary award; instead, the winning poet receives an honorarium of 20% of the total net royalties from all poetry books and chapbooks the press sold online in the year the winning book was published. The winner is also accorded the honor of being on the panel of judges for the next year's competition; all judges receive copies of all contending books to keep for their personal library.

www.ingramcontent.com/pod-product-compliance
Lightning Source LLC
Chambersburg PA
CBHW070010100426
42741CB00012B/3184